A LOOK AROUND

WASHINGTON, D.C.
OUR NATION'S CAPITAL

written by
Alison Strickland

photography by
Ted Coulson

Published by Willowisp Press, Inc., 10100 SBF Drive, Pinellas Park, Florida 34666
Copyright © 1985 by Willowisp Press, Inc.   All rights reserved.
Printed in the U.S.A.   ISBN 0-87406-047-8

CANAL RD.

C & O Canal

to National Zoo

29 WHITEHURST FREEWAY

KEY BRIDGE

CONNECTICUT AVE.

NEW HAMPSHIRE AVE.

PENNSYLVANIA AVE.

17TH ST.

Lafayette Park

GEORGE WASHINGTON MEMORIAL PKWY.

Little River

THEODORE ROOSEVELT ISLAND

ROCK CREEK & POTOMAC PKWY.

VIRGINIA AVE.

WHITE HOUSE

John F. Kennedy Center

The Ellipse

THEODORE ROOSEVELT BRIDGE 66

50 CONSTITUTION AVE.

Constitution Gardens

17TH ST.

ARLINGTON BLVD.

Marine Corps War Memorial

BACON DR.

Vietnam Veterans Memorial

Reflecting Pool

WASHINGTON MONUMENT

MARSHALL DR.

LINCOLN MEMORIAL

INDEPENDENCE

KUTZ BRIDGE

110

COLUMBIA

ARLINGTON MEMORIAL BRIDGE

WEST POTOMAC

OHIO DR.

PARK

Tidal Basin

ISLAND

Potomac

MEMORIAL DR.

JEFFERSON DAVIS HWY.

Boundary Channel

LADY BIRD JOHNSON

GEORGE WASHINGTON MEMORIAL PKWY.

River

Arlington House

Kennedy Grave Site

WASHINGTON BLVD.

Lyndon B. Johnson Memorial Grove

PARK

JEFFERSON MEMORIAL

ARLINGTON

NATIONAL

CEMETERY

Tomb of the Unknown Soldier

110

to Mount Vernon

395

395

1

1

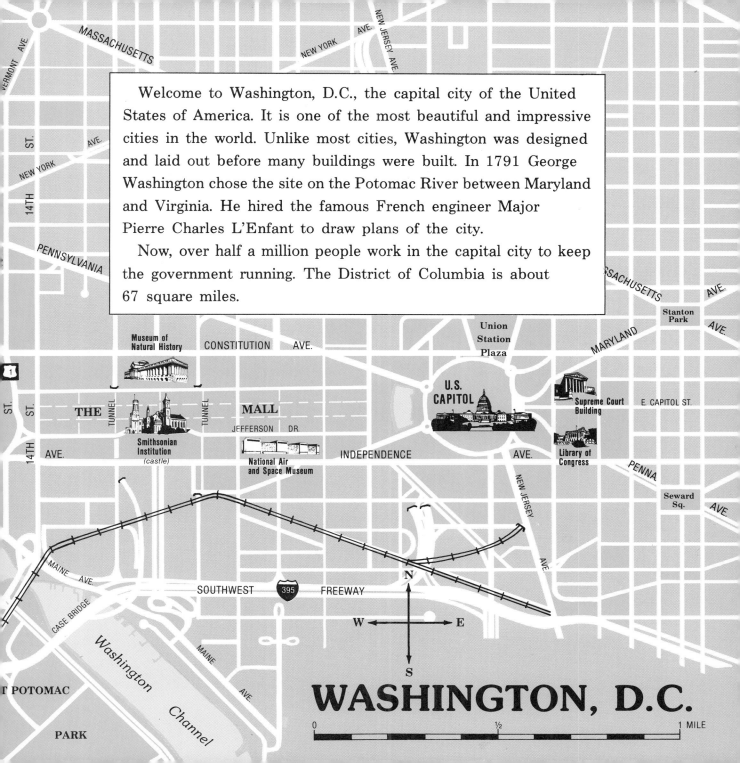

Welcome to Washington, D.C., the capital city of the United States of America. It is one of the most beautiful and impressive cities in the world. Unlike most cities, Washington was designed and laid out before many buildings were built. In 1791 George Washington chose the site on the Potomac River between Maryland and Virginia. He hired the famous French engineer Major Pierre Charles L'Enfant to draw plans of the city.

Now, over half a million people work in the capital city to keep the government running. The District of Columbia is about 67 square miles.

WASHINGTON, D.C.

0   ½   1 MILE

Congress meets in the Capitol building. Here, the senators and representatives that each state sends to Congress make the laws of the U.S. Inside is the Rotunda. This round hall is 96 feet across. Look up 183 feet into the dome, and you will see a painting of George Washington. This photograph shows the Capitol from East Capitol Street. Each newly elected President takes the oath of office during the Inauguration on these steps.

This is the Capitol from The Mall, on the west side. To the
left is the north wing where the Senate meets. To the right is the
south wing where the House of Representatives meets. A flag flying
above a wing means that house is in session. The lantern burning
above the Capitol dome at night means that Congress is in
night session. Atop the lantern stands the Statue of Freedom.

Walk down The Mall from the Capitol. Turn right at the Washington Monument. There you'll see the south side of the White House. The President's helicopter lands on the lawn behind the fountain. The children of presidents have run with their dogs, ridden their ponies and played in tree houses here. At Easter, Washington children are invited for the egg-rolling party on the White House lawn. The White House was built in 1800 and has been the home of every president except George Washington.

This is the White House from Pennsylvania Avenue. It is often called the Executive Mansion. Many dignitaries and famous people have walked through these front doors to visit with our U.S. presidents. Nearly every day news programs are broadcast from the lawn of the White House.

Millions of tourists visit the President's home every year. Guides give tours through the first floor. Visitors can see the east wing's famous rooms where presidents have held dinner parties, weddings, concerts, press conferences and funerals. Tourists can't go into the west wing. That is where the President has his offices. The second floor is closed to tourists because the President and his family live there.

At the opposite end of The Mall from the Capitol is the Lincoln Memorial. This memorial was built to honor one of America's best known presidents, Abraham Lincoln. It stands in West Potomac Park, a place where Lincoln liked to walk alone at night.

Lincoln led the U.S. through the Civil War. That war was fought between the northern and southern states. The 36 columns that surround the memorial stand for the states in the Union at the time of Lincoln's death. Lincoln was assassinated on April 14, 1865.

Veterans of all U.S. wars are buried in Arlington National Cemetery. Generals are buried next to privates and admirals next to seamen. Families of veterans also are buried here. On Memorial Day a small American flag is placed on each grave. Arlington is named for Arlington House, home of General Robert E. Lee, leader of the Confederate Army during the Civil War. The house is on a hill overlooking the cemetery. It is open to the public.

Down the hill from Arlington House is the Tomb of the Unknown Soldier. In the white marble tomb lies the body of a soldier killed in Europe during World War I. The soldier is called "unknown" because no one knows his name. In front of the tomb, two marble slabs mark the graves of unknown soldiers from W.W. II and the Korean conflict. The soldier standing to the right of the tomb is an honor guard. The tomb is guarded night and day.

The grave of President John F. Kennedy is located in Arlington National Cemetery. Above the simple marker burns the eternal flame, which was lit at Kennedy's burial. Near the grave site are Kennedy's famous words, "Ask not what your country can do for you. Ask what you can do for your country."

Not far from the entrance to Arlington National Cemetery is one of the most famous war memorials in Washington, D.C. It is the Marine Corps War Memorial. Many people call it the Iwo Jima Memorial.

This memorial represents the raising of the American flag on Mount Suribachi on the island of Iwo Jima during W.W. II. Over 6,800 Marines and 19,000 Japanese were killed in the Battle of Iwo Jima.

The statue was modeled after a well-known news photograph from W.W. II. The photograph was taken when the battle was won in 1945. Five Marines and a Navy hospital corpsman raised the U.S. flag. Iwo Jima was returned to Japan in 1968.

This monument of a flaming golden sword honors men who died in battle. Some of these men were members of the Second Division of the U.S. Army who died during W.W. I. The words under the sword say, "To our dead, 1917 – 1919." Later, the words honoring soldiers who died in W.W. II were carved on the left side of the monument. Those people who died in the Korean conflict were honored with words added on the right side. The monument is between the White House and the Washington Monument.

The Vietnam Veterans Memorial is located in Constitution Gardens. It is a wall shaped like a "V." One end points to the Washington Monument, the other to the Lincoln Memorial. Over 55,000 Americans, who were killed in Vietnam, have their names engraved on the wall. The names are listed according to date of death. When you visit the memorial you can see people looking for the name of someone they knew. Many visitors leave small flags or flowers below the name of a loved one.

NORTH

On a small hill in the middle of all the famous sights stands the
Washington Monument. It was built to honor George Washington.
You can see the 555-foot-tall monument from everywhere in
the city. You can take a 70-second elevator ride up to the
top of the monument and look out over the city. Look to
the north; you can see the White House. To the west is the
Lincoln Memorial and the Reflecting Pool. To the east lies the
Capitol and the Smithsonian buildings. To the south, the Jefferson
Memorial overlooks the Tidal Basin.

WEST

EAST

The monument's cornerstone was laid on the Fourth of July in 1848. The monument took 50 years to build. Construction was stopped once by lack of money, and later by the start of the Civil War. Different colors of stone mark the stops in construction. Building blocks for the monument were donated by clubs and organizations from all over America and from foreign countries like China, Greece, and Japan. Each Fourth of July is celebrated with gigantic fireworks displays on the monument grounds. This is a national landmark.

SOUTH

The Jefferson Memorial honors the third president of the U.S., Thomas Jefferson. He was only 33 years old when he wrote the Declaration of Independence. The statue inside the memorial shows him standing before the committee that asked him to write the Declaration. Quotations from Jefferson's famous writings are engraved on the walls around his statue.

The cherry trees planted around the Jefferson Memorial and the Tidal Basin were a gift from Tokyo, Japan.

This is the Supreme Court building, home of the highest court in the U.S. The first court met in 1790. The Supreme Court consists of nine judges. Their job is to decide if the laws go against the Constitution. If the judges decide a law is unconstitutional, that law will not go into effect. When the court meets, the judges shake hands. This tradition shows that the judges will work together to preserve freedom. Over the giant bronze doors is the inscription, "Equal justice under law."

All around Washington you can find memorials of people who have made great contributions to our country. The Albert Einstein Memorial is in front of the National Academy of Sciences. The bronze statue of this famous scientist is three times life size, but Einstein looks human, warm, and friendly. Einstein is famous because of the discoveries he made about time and light and their effects on the universe.

The floor in front of his statue shows the stars and planets of the universe. Einstein's work helped make space travel possible. That's why this crystal etching of him is in the National Air and Space Museum at the Smithsonian Institution.

This Smithsonian museum was opened in 1976. The Smithsonian Institute Museums line the grassy Mall between the Washington Monument and the Capitol.

The double-winged plane above is the "flying machine" the Wright Brothers flew at Kitty Hawk, North Carolina, in 1903. Above it to the right is *The Spirit of St. Louis* which Charles Lindbergh flew across the Atlantic to Paris, France. These two planes were the beginning of modern aviation. You will also see the *Bell X-1,* the first plane to fly faster than sound.

The Air and Space Museum also has unusual kites, gliders and balloons. People experimented with kites before planes were invented.

On the ground floor of the museum are the more recent spacecraft. You can see the space capsules the first astronauts flew and a duplicate of the lunar landing module that the Apollo II astronauts landed on the moon. You

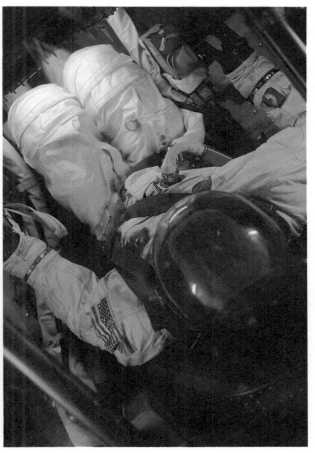

can also touch a moon rock and see a planetarium show. You can feel like you're flying as you watch movies on a giant screen. This is one of the greatest aerospace centers of the world.

Across the street from the Supreme Court building is the Library of Congress. Inside are so many books, maps, films, photographs and records that computers are used to keep track of the huge collections. Congressmen use the library to find information. It is also open to the public. The library and the Capitol are connected by a book tunnel, a system that carries books to and from the halls. Inside on the main floor you can see one copy of the Gutenberg Bible, the first book ever printed.

A visit to the C & O (Chesapeake and Ohio) Canal is like a trip back in time. Tourists can ride the canal boats through the locks that raise and lower the water level between waterways. The people who operate the locks and guide the boats are dressed like early American settlers. Mules pull the boats. The canal was dug along the north bank of the Potomac River. George Washington wanted the canal built so boats could travel past the waterfalls at Great Falls, Virginia. It was completed in 1850.

This is Mount Vernon, the restored home of George Washington. It sits on a hill overlooking the Potomac River about 15 miles south of Washington, D.C. Every time a U.S. Navy ship passes Mount Vernon, the flag is lowered. Then the ship's bell is rung and the crew stands at attention. This ceremony is in honor of Washington who is buried there in a simple tomb. Visitors can walk through the main house and see many things that belonged to the Washingtons. The kitchen is connected to the house by a covered walkway. It looks like it did over 200 years ago.

Washington moved to Mount Vernon when he was 22. Soon he married Martha. George liked farming his plantation. He had slaves who helped him. The slave quarters are near the house.

When the Revolutionary War (1775-1781) started, Washington was made commander-in-chief of the American army. In 1789 he became the first president of the United States. He and Martha moved to New York City, the first seat of government. After two

terms as President, he went back to Mount Vernon. Two years later, in 1799, he died there at age 67. His slaves were freed when he died. Washington had lived at Mount Vernon only 16 years.

These kids are playing on a Triceratops prorsus, a prehistoric creature that invites you into the Museum of Natural History, located on The Mall. This Smithsonian museum contains skeletons of dinosaurs. There's also a giant 8-ton mounted African elephant, the largest on record. It is also the home of the Hope Diamond which weighs 45.5 carats. This beautiful diamond was thought to bring bad luck to anyone who owned it. You can also see mummies, American Indian exhibits, and an insect zoo.

The National Zoo, a 20-minute ride from The Mall, is another part of the Smithsonian. This is a place where animals are studied. The most famous animals are Ling-Ling and Hsing-Hsing. These giant pandas were a gift from China. You can watch seals, otters and polar bears play under water. Birds from around the world are kept in the Great Flight Cage. You can visit gorillas in the Great Ape House. Visitors can see unusual animals from around the world.

Above: A and C, statues in front of the Supreme Court building; *B,* statue of Thomas Jefferson; *D,* First Division Memorial; *E,* figure from the Ulysses S. Grant Memorial in front of the Capitol; *F,* the sculpture *Infinity* in front of the National Museum of American History.

Right: G, Washington Monument; *H,* National Christmas Tree; *I,* fireworks above The Mall.

G

H

I

31

INDEX

The page numbers in bold face refer to photographs.